BRITISH HISTORY MAKERS
WILLIAM SHAKESPEARE

LEON ASHWORTH

CHERRYTREE BOOKS

A Cherrytree Book

Designed and produced by
A S Publishing

First published 1997
by Cherrytree Press Ltd
a subsidiary of
The Chivers Company Ltd
Windsor Bridge Road
Bath BA2 3AX

© Cherrytree Press Ltd 1997

British Library Cataloguing in Publication Data

Ashworth, Leon
    William Shakespeare. – (British history makers)
    1.Shakespeare, William, 1564-1616 – Juvenile literature
    2. Dramatists, English – Early modern, 1500-1700 – Biography –
        Juvenile literature
    I.Title
    822.3'3

ISBN 0 7451 5292 9 (Hardcover)
ISBN 0 7540 9015 9 (Softcover)

Printed and bound in Italy by New Interlitho, Milan.

Acknowledgments

Design: Richard Rowan
Editorial: John Grisewood
Artwork: Malcolm Porter
Photographs: *Barnaby's Picture Library* 4 bottom, 7 centre, 8 top & centre, 11
centre, 11 bottom (Courtesy of the Marquess of Salisbury), 15 bottom, 16
centre & bottom, 17 bottom left, 19 top & bottom right, 24 bottom, 25
bottom *The Bridgeman Art Library* 4 top, 9 centre, 9 bottom & back
cover (British Library, London), 10/11 top (The Royal Cornwall
Museum, Truro), 14 bottom, 19 bottom left (Dulwich Picture Gallery),
20 bottom & front cover, 23 top (Woburn Abbey, Bedfordshire)
& bottom (Forbes Magazine Collection, New York), 24 bottom
left (Victoria & Albert Museum, London), 25 centre, 26
bottom left (British Library, London), 28 bottom left *Corpus
Christi College, Cambridge (Courtesy of the Masters and
Fellows)* 17 bottom right *Dulwich Picture Gallery (By
permission of the trustees)* 12 left *e. t. archive* 13 centre, 20 top
Fitzwilliam Museum, University of Cambridge 12/13 bottom
Hulton Getty 21 centre *Jarrold Publishing* 26/27 centre, 27
bottom *The Mansell Collection* 6 top, 13 top, 21 bottom *Mary Evans Picture
Library* 16/17 top, 28 top, 29 top *National Portrait Gallery* 5 & cover
portrait, 18 left, 22 top *Public Record Office* 27 right *The Ronald Grant
Archive* 28 bottom right *Shakespeare's Globe/Richard Kalina* 29 centre &
bottom *Zefa* 6 bottom

CONTENTS

■ SHAKESPEARE – MAN OF THE THEATRE

WILLIAM SHAKESPEARE grew up in the England of Queen Elizabeth I and wrote his plays when the theatre was new. Now, more than 400 years later, these same plays still fill theatres with people who laugh at the jokes, cry at the sad parts, and marvel that one person could understand so much about human nature.

Shakespeare's was an exciting time to live. New ideas were in the air. There were new books to read. People were ready to fight over the rights and wrongs of religion. Travellers brought back tales of wonder from newly found lands overseas. Sailors told of their adventures in the Indies, Africa and America.

It was also a time when the wealthy and high-born took a keen interest in poetry, in art and in music. Famous adventurers and soldiers, such as Sir Walter Raleigh and Sir Philip Sidney, wrote poetry. Other wealthy people helped poets and artists by becoming their patrons – they paid and protected them.

Shakespeare's way of writing was new, too. Just seven years before he was born, the Earl of Surrey made up a new form of verse to turn Latin poems into English. It was called blank verse, and Shakespeare used blank verse for most of his plays.

Crowds flocked to the first theatres in Elizabeth's reign – and to keep them coming, the theatres needed new plays. William Shakespeare wrote them, and so successfully that they have kept the theatre alive to this day.

SHAKESPEARE'S LIFE

1564 Shakespeare born
1582 Marries Anne Hathaway
1583 Daughter Susanna born
1585 Twins Hamnet and Judith born
1590 By now Shakespeare has left Stratford for London
1596 Son Hamnet dies
1597 Buys New Place in Stratford
1616 Shakespeare dies

▲ The poet Shakespeare dreams by the fire and, in this Victorian artist's fantasy, conjures out of the flames some of his best-known characters.

▼ Shakespeare's signature; one of six known examples, all of which are different. Experts claim that he used the spelling 'Shakspere'.

■ THE SHAKESPEARE FAMILY ■

SHAKESPEARE'S BIRTH date is not known. He was christened in the church at Stratford-upon-Avon, Warwickshire, on 26 April 1564, when probably about three days old. Young William had a comfortable home in Henley Street. His father, John, was a glove-maker. His mother, Mary, was the daughter of a local farmer called Robert Arden.

SISTERS AND BROTHERS

William was the Shakespeares' first son. Two girls born before him both died in childhood. After him came two more sisters and three brothers. One of these sisters also died, aged eight. Edmund, the last brother, was born when William was 16.

A FATHER OF SOME IMPORTANCE

John Shakespeare was an important man in Stratford. Although he had once been fined for having a dunghill (rubbish dump) in front of his house, he had risen to a seat on the town council and was bailiff (mayor) when William was four. He may have had several business interests and certainly owned more than one house in the town. His own father, Richard, had been a farmer, renting land from the father of Mary Arden.

▲ The entry in the church register that records Shakespeare's christening is dated 26 April 1564, and his birthday is traditionally celebrated on 23 April.

▶ The font at which Shakespeare was christened is still in Holy Trinity Church, Stratford-upon-Avon. His father was an important man in the town so the family would have sat near the front at Sunday services.

▶ A plan of the house in Henley Street (far right) where Shakespeare was born. His father's trade in leather goods, wool and farm products was profitable enough for him to buy two houses in Stratford.

▼ Mary Arden's house at Wilmcote near Stratford. William's mother came from an old landowning family. She married John Shakespeare shortly after inheriting part of her father's property.

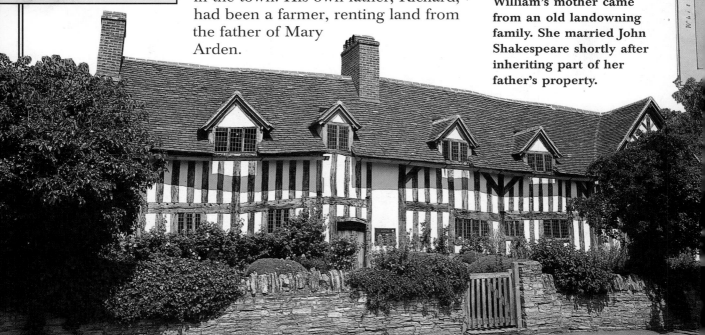

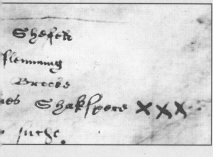

THE SHAKESPEARE CHILDREN

Joan, born 1558; dies before 1569, when another Joan is christened.
Margaret, born 1562; dies 1563.
William, born 1564; dies aged 52.

Joan, christened 1569; marries William Hart, a hat-maker; dies aged 77.
Gilbert, born 1566; dies aged 45.
Anne, born 1571; dies 1579.
Richard, born 1574; dies aged 38.
Edmund, born 1580; an actor; dies aged 27.

Town records tell us that John Shakespeare was a borough taster in 1556, with the job of inspecting Stratford's bread and ale. He also served for a time as constable, keeping law and order in the town, and was made an alderman (senior councillor) in 1565, soon after William was born. When plague struck Stratford around this time, the council met outdoors in an orchard – where they hoped to be safe from catching the deadly sickness.

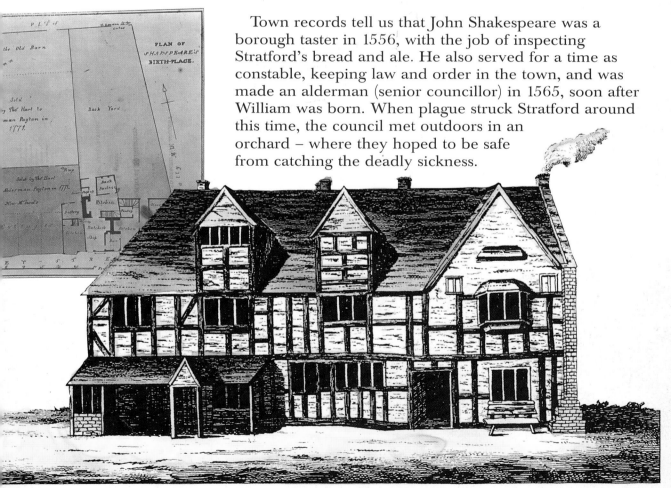

■ SCHOOLDAYS AND AFTER ■

JOHN SHAKESPEARE, as an alderman, had the honour of wearing a fur-trimmed gown at big town events. He could also claim a free place for his son at the local grammar school. The schoolmaster, paid for by the council, taught the boys Latin, Greek, ancient history and rhetoric (the art of speech-making). Young Will would already have learned his alphabet from a 'hornbook' and his mother may have taught him how to read and write.

▲ Bowls, or ninepins, was a popular game of skittles enjoyed by people of all classes.

▶ Twelfth Night – the last day of Christmas – was a time for revels and feasts.

EVENTS

1569 *The Queen's Players perform in Stratford's Guild Hall.*
1571 *A law requires all people over the age of seven in England to wear a woollen cap on Sundays – this is to boost trade for wool traders and cap-makers. Ottoman Turks lose sea battle of Lepanto to Don John of Austria.*
1572 *Government declares actors must be counted as 'sturdy beggars' unless licensed or under a lord's protection. The playwright Ben Jonson and poet John Donne are born. In France, over 20,000 Protestants (known as Huguenots) are killed in the St Bartholomew's Day Massacre.*

SPELL AS YOU LIKE IT

The grammar taught at Tudor grammar schools was Latin (the language of scholars throughout Europe). Anyone hoping for a career in the church, law or teaching had to read and write Latin correctly, but English did not follow such strict rules. Its spelling was not yet fixed, and people wrote words as they heard them.

School was hard work. The hours were long, holidays were few, and boys

▲ This may have bee Shakespeare's schoolroom, but in h day there would have been no rows of desk Only the master had desk. The boys sat or benches and wrote o slates on their laps.

◀ Discipline was har in Tudor schools. Boy found playing about like these ones would have been beaten.

8

who did not know their lessons were beaten. The playwright Ben Jonson said that the adult Shakespeare 'knew small Latin and less Greek'. The young Shakespeare may not have cared for the grammar of the ancient Greeks and Romans, but he liked their stories. Years later, he used them as plots for his plays.

FUN OUT OF SCHOOL

When not at school, young Will probably helped in the house and workshop. Perhaps he ran messages for his father, or visited his mother's farming relatives. There were country festivals and town fairs, the River Avon for swimming and fishing, and visits by strolling players or entertainers.

In 1569, the Queen's Players came to perform in Stratford's Guild Hall. They were a band of actors who performed 'Interludes', a mixture of long, high-flown speeches, funny cross-talk and slapstick comedy. Five-year-old Will Shakespeare may well have been allowed to watch their performances.

STROLLING PLAYERS

IN THE Middle Ages, people enjoyed plays put on by the craft guilds (such as the shoemakers or goldsmiths). These plays were Bible stories acted in the church porch or outside on a cart. By the time Shakespeare was a child, bands of actors and entertainers (below) were touring from town to town. Among them were clowns, acrobats, jugglers, singers and dancers. Some were regarded as little more than roving louts or beggars, but others were respectable. They performed in inn-yards, market places and streets, and sometimes in the halls of great houses. These actors usually had a nobleman as their patron and wore his livery (uniform). The best companies were famed countrywide – and even abroad.

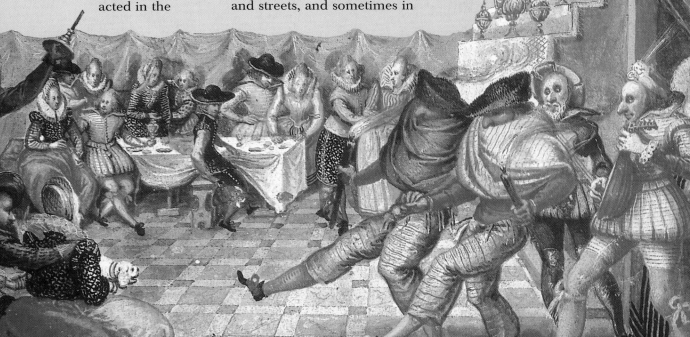

■ MEETING THE PLAYERS ■

IN 1575, WHEN Will was 11, Stratford buzzed with excitement over Queen Elizabeth's visit to the Earl of Leicester at nearby Kenilworth Castle. For three weeks the queen's favourite courtier entertained her with dazzling displays of pageantry. News of the spectacular events no doubt prompted the Shakespeare family to walk from Stratford and see for themselves.

Will would not have been disappointed. The queen had brought her entire court. There was hunting and feasting; plays, pageants and masques on the castle lawns; fireworks at night; cannon-shooting by day; music, poetry and dancing. A display on the lake featured Orion the Hunter carrying off the Lady of the Lake on a dolphin.

Noble lords and ladies enjoyed dressing up to take part in pageants and masques. But the Earl of Leicester also had his own company of actors. Its leader was James Burbage, who in London was soon to open the first public theatre in England.

▲ A visit by Queen Elizabeth to nearby Kenilworth Castle would have been an occasion for everyone to remember. For most ordinary local people it would have been a once-in-a-lifetime chance to glimpse the splendour of the monarch and her courtiers.

▼ Anne Hathaway's Cottage at Shottery near Stratford was the farmhouse in which Shakespeare's wife lived before their marriage. This event took place by special licence soon after the death of her father. The licence allowed couples to marry without the customary calling of banns.

CHANGING CIRCUMSTANCES

By 1580 Will Shakespeare had left school. His young sister Anne had just died and his last brother Edmund was newly born. Family life was not so easy now. John Shakespeare had money problems. He sold land, was excused paying taxes and lost his place on the town council. William did not go to university. He may have found work as a teacher or in a lawyer's office, or with his father. He had to earn money somehow, for in 1582 at the age of 18 he was married and a year later he was a father.

Will's wife, Anne Hathaway, was a farmer's daughter and eight years older than her husband. Their first child was called Susanna. Twins were born two years later in 1585, a girl, Judith, and a boy, Hamnet.

▼ Servants prepare a feast as musicians play and wedding guests stroll and chat. This picture, called A Fête at Bermondsey, is by the Dutch painter Hoefnagel.

NOBLE COMPANY OF ACTORS

IN 1572, the government passed a law for the 'Punishment of Vagabonds'. In future, such wanderers as pedlars, jugglers, tinkers (pot-menders), chapmen (street sellers), fencers (sword-fighters) and common players (actors) would be treated as 'sturdy beggars'. This meant that they could be whipped back to their home parish (above), unless they had a licence or were employed by a nobleman. Players rushed to join the professional acting companies of a nobleman and wear his livery.

SEEKING HIS FORTUNE

THE EARL OF Leicester was not the only nobleman with his own company of actors. The earls of Worcester, Warwick and Berkeley all had companies that performed in Stratford while Shakespeare was there. Worcester's men had by far the finest actor, Edward Alleyn, who was just two years younger than Shakespeare. Perhaps while watching or talking to the players – helping or writing something topical about Stratford for them – young Will discovered that performing plays was what he wanted to do. But where was he to do it? And how?

JOINING A COMPANY

Sometime in the late 1580s, William Shakespeare decided to leave Stratford and seek his fortune in London, as others had done before him. He

◄ Edward Alleyn, the finest actor of his day. He owned several theatres and organized bull- and bear-baiting events. He made so much money that he was able to found Dulwich College school.

▶ On the bank of the River Thames at Richmond, morris dancers perform and collect money from wealthy passers-by.

CLOWN AND JESTER

YOUNG Shakespeare in Stratford probably laughed when he saw the clown Richard Tarlton (right) poking his head around a curtain, cross-eyed and pulling faces, or capering about playing a pipe and tabor (small drum). Like all writers, Will later made use of his memories in his work. When he first came to London, Tarlton may still have been on the stage. He was a favourite court jester of Queen Elizabeth and many of his tricks were copied by later clowns. Tarlton died in 1588. It is probable that he was recalled by Shakespeare as Yorick, the dead jester in *Hamlet* who had made the young prince laugh.

may have left with an acting company. The Queen's Men who played in Stratford in 1587 had just lost an actor, killed in a stabbing. Two of their other players were famous comedians: the young Will Kemp and Richard Tarlton, a clown and entertainer near the end of his career. Will Shakespeare may have joined them as an apprentice.

LEAVING FOR THE CITY

Very little is known about Shakespeare's life at this time. For years there was a story that he fled Stratford after being caught poaching deer from Sir Thomas Lucy. Few people now believe this. Other tales tell of him working in Gloucestershire as a tutor to the Earl of Berkeley's children, or as a soldier abroad. All we do know is that by 1592, William Shakespeare was making his living by writing plays in London.

▶ A map of London, drawn in 1572, shows its densely packed streets, and river busy with traffic.

■ THE ROAD TO LONDON ■

SHAKESPEARE travelled the road between Stratford and London many times. Journeys then were on horseback or on foot. Only the queen and the very rich had carriages. People rested and ate at wayside inns, if they could afford to. Others found or begged shelter where they could.

A MAGNET FOR ALL SORTS

When young Will reached London in the 1580s, he found a crowded, dirty city that was full of life, sounds and action. It was a busy port, huddled beside the River Thames, its streets thronged with people of all sorts and trades. Trade was nowhere brisker than in the ale-houses, where inn-keepers found entertainers good for business. Plays and mimes (called dumb-shows) were acted in the yards of city taverns, but the crowds they attracted also brought pickpockets and cutpurses, drunkards and beggars.

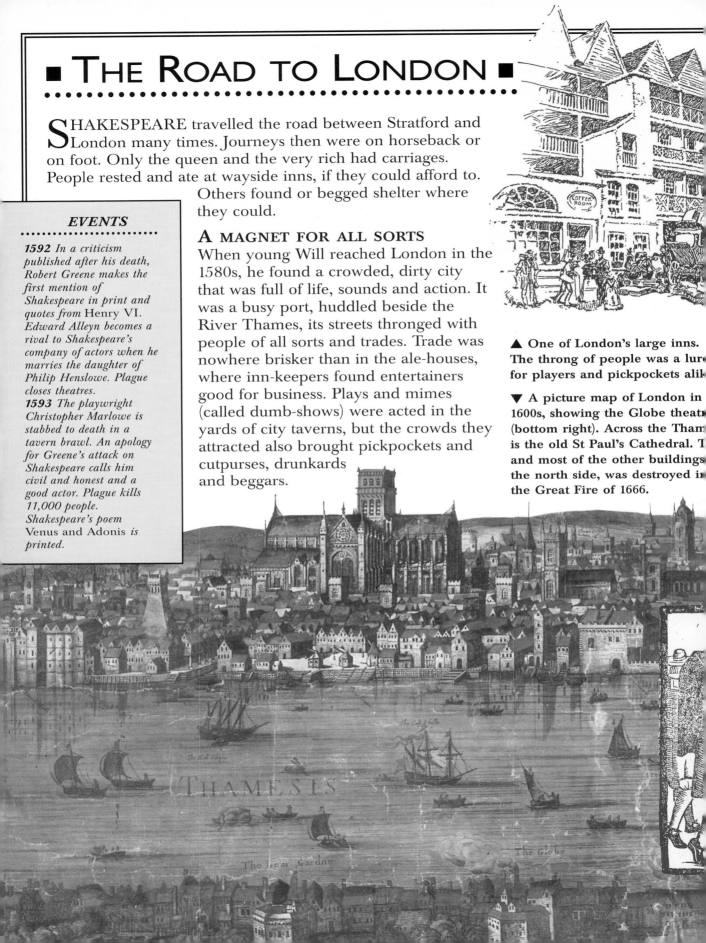

▲ One of London's large inns. The throng of people was a lure for players and pickpockets alike

▼ A picture map of London in 1600s, showing the Globe theatre (bottom right). Across the Thames is the old St Paul's Cathedral. This and most of the other buildings on the north side, was destroyed in the Great Fire of 1666.

A BUMPY RIDE

WHEN Queen Elizabeth travelled about her kingdom, she took with her 400 wagons full of belongings. Poor people went with their goods in heavy wooden carts pulled by up to ten horses. Tudor coaches had no springs and were very uncomfortable – the queen rode in one only when entering a town. Most travellers hired horses at each inn they stopped at. Roads were rarely mended and ruts made by cart wheels were so deep that people sometimes fell into them and drowned. Carts often turned over. There were no road signs and farmers sometimes ploughed across the highway. Nobody dared travel at night for fear of robbers hiding in the woods. When they stopped at inns, they were preyed upon by cutpurses (right).

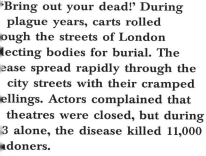

'Bring out your dead!' During plague years, carts rolled [thr]ough the streets of London [col]lecting bodies for burial. The [dis]ease spread rapidly through the city streets with their cramped [dw]ellings. Actors complained that theatres were closed, but during [159]3 alone, the disease killed 11,000 [Lon]doners.

A DANGER TO MORALS AND HEALTH

Plays, according to the strict, religious Puritans, were 'the nest of the Devil and the sink of all sin'. London's Lord Mayor also thought plays were dangerous because of 'sundry slaughters and maimings of the queen's subjects, that have happened by falling scaffolds, frames and stages, and by engines, weapons and powder used in plays'. Special effects obviously went wrong! Crowded audiences were breeding grounds, too, for the plague and other diseases.

LONDON'S NEW THEATRES

When plague struck London in hot summers, all performances of plays were stopped and the actors left town to tour the country. Complaints about the players and their rowdy audiences soon brought more rules and regulations from the Lord Mayor. Life became so difficult for actors in the city that they decided to move outside it.

James Burbage, actor to the Earl of Leicester and the queen, rented some ground in grassy Shoreditch and there built a 'plaie howse' of wood. Burbage, a trained carpenter, called it the Theatre (short for amphitheatre) and opened it in 1576. It did so well that the following year another playhouse, called the Curtain, opened nearby. Soon a rival playhouse, the Rose, was opened by Philip Henslowe. When Shakespeare came to London, these theatres were all thriving.

■ ACTOR AND PLAYWRIGHT ■

SHAKESPEARE probably learned his acting skills with Burbage's company at the Theatre. There was also a story that he began work in London *outside* the theatre — looking after the horses of rich members of the audience while they were inside watching the play!

Playgoers making for the Rose theatre crossed the Thames by ferry. Nearby stood the Bear Garden, where people watched mastiff dogs set upon a bear or a bull tied to a post. Other popular sports were cock-fighting, wrestling and bowls matches. Archers shot at targets at the butts, in fields near the city.

Rival attractions like these made theatres work hard to keep their customers. Besides plays, they put on variety and circus acts, and often ended the entertainment with a 'jig' — a knockabout farce with jokes, cross-talk, topical satire and spirited dancing presented by the clowns.

HITS OF THE DAY
Acting companies sent spies to watch

▼ **Most people today are sickened by the idea of animal-baiting (right) but, in Shakespeare's day, crowds flocked to the bull- and bear-baiting rings. They also enjoyed violence in plays.**

THE THEATRE

PUBLIC theatres like the Swan (above) put on show in the daytime only. The buildings were round, square many sided, and open to the sky. Most had three-tiered galleries built round a courtya known as the pit. Customers stood in the pit, or paid extra sit on benches in the galleries The standing spectators were called groundlings. At one en the apron stage jutted out ove the pit. Actors came and wen through doorways at the bacl the stage. Behind these were dressing rooms. The stage ha trap door (through which dev

The Bancke

The bolle bayting

The Beare bayting

teltum

iue arena.

new plays put on by their rivals. They wrote down as much as they could of the words and plot in shorthand and then produced their own 'pirate' version. Shakespeare probably saw many of the new plays written by clever young men called the 'university wits'. Their pieces mixed poetry and low comedy, romance and rhetoric. The best plays were those by Christopher Marlowe, whose *Tamburlaine*, *The Jew of Malta* and *Dr Faustus* were all acted by Edward Alleyn. Marlowe's friend Thomas Kyd wrote a popular play called *The Spanish Tragedy*. Audiences loved this tale of horror, with its ghosts, gory murders, torture and madness.

A NEW AUTHOR MAKES A MARK

Some of these early playwrights led dangerous, violent lives themselves. Marlowe, a spy in the government's secret service, was killed in a tavern brawl. His friend and fellow playwright Robert Greene kept company with thieves and vagabonds, and died in poverty. Just before his death in 1592, Greene warned playwrights against a newcomer – an 'upstart crow' who thought himself able to write blank verse as well as the university men. He was 'in his own conceit the only "Shakes-scene" in a country'. Greene was writing about William Shakespeare.

In 1592, Philip Henslowe put on a new play – *Harry the Sixth* – at the Rose. It made more money than anything else played all season. We know the play as Shakespeare's *Henry VI*. Shakespeare the actor was now a playwright.

▼ A page from the prompt book for *Titus Andronicus* shows the costumes that actors wore in Shakespeare's time.

▼ This may be a portrait of Christopher Marlowe, the greatest English playwright before Shakespeare.

nd ghosts could appear and isappear). Sound and other pecial effects were worked om the hut, which stood on op of the 'heavens', a half-roof ver the stage. Machinery inside ould let down an actor from e 'sky'. There was no curtain r scenery, but actors did use rops such as crowns, swords, rniture and artificial trees hich were kept in the tiring-ouse on each tier. To advertise e play, a flag was hoisted over e theatre to show that a erformance would take place the afternoon. To announce e start, there was much owing of trumpets, ringing of lls and banging of drums.

■ PLAYS AND PLAYERS ■

SHAKESPEARE had probably written his first plays by 1589-90, perhaps while still learning the actor's trade. Among the earliest were *The Comedy of Errors*, *The Taming of the Shrew* and *Richard III*. Then in 1593 plague struck London. The theatres were shut and many players left to tour the country or act abroad. Shakespeare seems to have stayed in the city and, as no new plays were needed, he wrote poems instead. Poets in Elizabethan England commanded more respect than playwrights.

EVENTS

1596 Shakespeare's son Hamnet dies. The Shakespeares gain a coat of arms. The Swan theatre is built on the south bank of the Thames, seating 3000. Shakespeare is involved in a lawsuit. Drake dies in the West Indies. Edmund Spenser publishes his epic poem The Faerie Queene. *1597* Ben Jonson begins acting and writing. James Burbage dies. Shakespeare buys New Place in Stratford. A new Poor Law makes parishes responsible for looking after the local poor. Rebellion in Ireland.

PUBLISHED POEMS

Shakespeare wrote two long poems, *Venus and Adonis* and *The Rape of Lucrece*. He dedicated them both to the young Earl of Southampton, probably in return for gifts of money. Both were printed by Richard Field, a neighbour from Stratford who was now a printer in London. These poems were the only works by Shakespeare that he published himself.

◀ The Earl of Southampton was Shakespeare's patron, though nobody knows exactly how much money he paid to the poet or how well the two men knew each other. It is possible that Shakespeare lived in his household for a time.

▶ A list made in Shakespeare's day of some of the actors who performed in his plays.

SHAKESPEARE'S ACTOR

THERE were no actresses in Shakespeare's day. All parts were taken by men, with boys or youths playing women and children. Companies had around eight to twelve 'sharers' who ran the business and were the leading actors. They employed hirelings to do odd jobs, play music or act as prompts (whispering the next line if an actor forgot his words). The Lord Chamberlain's Men were originally Will Kemp and Thomas Pope (both clowns), John Heminges, Augustine Phillips and George Bryan. Burbage and Shakespeare then joined them. Kemp probably played Bottom the Weaver in *A Midsummer Night's Dream*.

▼ The clown Robert Armin had a good voice, so Shakespeare wrote songs for him to sing in the plays.

HAKESPEARE'S ONNETS

HAKESPEARE was a superb poet. He wrote a ries of 154 short poems, or nnets, before 1600. A sonnet is poem of 14 lines, and many mous people of Shakespeare's ay, such as Sir Philip Sidney nd Sir Walter Raleigh, wrote nnets. Among Shakespeare's ost famous is the one that egins *'Shall I compare thee to a mmer's day . . .'* The first 126 nnets are addressed to a young bleman; the rest are pparently written to a woman. e do not know who these eople were. The sonnets were inted in 1609.

Richard Burbage.

A drawing of New Place, hakespeare's house in ratford. The building self has long gone.

BACK IN BUSINESS

In 1594 the theatres opened again. Shakespeare's fellow actors regrouped and found a new patron: the Lord Chamberlain. In October 1594 they opened at the Theatre in Shoreditch, led by Richard Burbage, son of James. Shakespeare was now an important member of the Lord Chamberlain's Men, a 'sharer' (shareholder) taking part of the profits. He worked hard, producing about two plays a year. All were written to suit the members of the company – with parts for each actor.

HEROES AND CLOWNS

Richard Burbage took the leads as Hamlet, Othello, Macbeth or King Lear. Comic parts went to Will Kemp until he left the company in 1599. This cheerful clown, singer and dancer had played in the lively comedies *A Midsummer Night's Dream* and *Much Ado About Nothing*. For Kemp's replacement, Robert Armin, Shakespeare wrote more thoughtful parts in *As You Like It* and *Twelfth Night*. Even in his tragedies, Shakespeare wrote funny scenes for his leading comic to play.

A 'GENTLEMAN'

By 1598, Shakespeare had written over a dozen plays. They were performed for the queen at court, as well as in the theatre, and made him wealthy enough to buy New Place – the second-biggest house in Stratford. It cost him £60 in 1597. A year earlier, he had helped his father pay for a coat of arms and with it the formal status of a 'gentleman'. The actor and playwright was now entitled to be called Mr Shakespeare. But the honour would not pass to William's son, for in August 1596, young Hamnet Shakespeare died.

■ AROUND THE GLOBE ■

THE LORD Chamberlain's Men were soon London's most successful company, but they badly needed a new building. Their lease on the Theatre was running out. At last, the company found a new site at Bankside in Southwark. In the bitter cold of Christmas 1598, they tore down the old Theatre building and carted its timbers across the frozen Thames.

The new theatre was London's finest. Large enough to hold perhaps 2500 people, it was round so the actors named it the Globe. On the flag that fluttered from its roof was the motto (in Latin) 'All the world's a stage'.

GLOBE. SOUTHWARKE.

INSIDE THE GLOBE

The flag was raised as a sign that a performance would take place that afternoon, starting at 2 o'clock. Each play was performed for a few days, and then replaced with a new one – though it would be brought back later if audiences liked it. People paid a penny to enter the theatre, and around the entrance were sideshows where jugglers, fortune-tellers, apple-sellers and quack doctors

▼ **Hogarth's painting of Sir John Falstaff, one of Shakespeare's most popular characters.**

▲ **The Globe theatre opened with a performance of *Henry V*. The Lord Chamberlain's Men owned the theatre.**

HOW ACTORS SPOKE AND ACTED

SHAKESPEARE'S actors probably spoke quickly, in a clear, musical style. They would not have sounded like actors today. The actors' accents included ones that may have sounded like those of Lancashire, America or Ireland today. 'Love' and 'above', for example, rhymed with 'prove' and 'move', and the *ea* sound in 'reason' sounded like the *ea* in 'steak'.

There were no drama schools, so actors learned from one another; set gestures (above)

reinforced their words. A clenched fist indicated pain, a scratched head puzzlement and so on.

touted for more coins.

Inside, the audience chatted cheerfully as they waited for the trumpet blast that signalled the start of the play. Playhouses were noisy. Audiences clapped what they liked and 'mewed' what they did not. After the play came the jig – comic turns and dancing.

On the stage of the Globe, Shakespeare's greatest plays had their first performances. He had been writing more about English history, creating in *Henry IV* (Parts 1 & 2) the part of the fat, drunken Sir John Falstaff – a great favourite with audiences and with Queen Elizabeth.

A FAMILY FRIENDSHIP

Like the theatre, Shakespeare too seems to have moved. For some years he lodged in the house of a Huguenot (French Protestant) family called Mountjoy in Silver Street, Cripplegate. Maybe he found them helpful with the French spoken in the Globe's opening play, *Henry V*. If so, Shakespeare returned the favour by helping the Mountjoys arrange a marriage for their daughter. We know this because in 1612, he was asked to give evidence when a dispute over the wedding agreement came to court. Shakespeare's evidence favoured neither one side nor the other. People seem to have found him a 'gentle' (meaning polite and tactful) man.

Ben Jonson was a friend and admirer of Shakespeare, and the two men acted in each other's plays.

Will Kemp, accompanied by his piper Thomas Sly, soon left the Globe. He laid a bet that he would dance all the way from London to Norwich. 'Kemp's jig' took nine days. Crowds watched him pass; he gained the freedom of Norwich, a life pension, and wrote a book. Following this success he left England to dance on the Continent, returning in 1602 to act for the Earl of Worcester's Men.

■ THE KING'S MEN ■

MANY OF Shakespeare's plays, even those about English or Roman history, refer to topical events and famous people of the day. Sometimes the players themselves were caught up in these events. Queen Elizabeth was growing old. The Earl of Essex, her former favourite, felt himself badly treated by the queen and government after failing on a mission to Ireland. In 1601, Essex led a revolt. On the day of the uprising, his supporters paid the Lord Chamberlain's Men to act Shakespeare's *Richard II*, a play about a king's overthrow. The revolt failed. Essex was beheaded. The actors were questioned, but not punished.

A MAN OF SUBSTANCE

Old John Shakespeare died the same year (1601), having lived to see his son restore the family fortune and honour by the skill of his pen. William inherited the house in Henley Street.

▲ **King James I.**

TRICKS OF THE TRADE

AUDIENCES loved exciting special effects, such as sparks and thunderbolts, cannon, drums, flags, fights and processions. The shouts and trumpet of a stage battle could be heard across the river! Actors dressed behind the stage. They put on wigs and make-up – flour to whiten the face, ink to draw lines, brick-dust for red cheeks, burnt cork and charcoal for black faces and shadows. Blood came from the butcher, and splendid costumes were often bought secondhand from noblemen and women. A property list of Philip Henslowe's includes: '1 lion skin; 1 bear's skin; Neptune's fork and garland; Kent's wooden leg'. It also includes a 'frame for the heading' – trick machinery for making it look as though an actor's head had been cut off!

BOY-ACTORS

THERE were two famous all-boy acting companies: the Children of St Paul's and the Children of the Chapel Royal. As well as performing plays, they were choirboys, singing and reciting verses at court. In fact, they became serious rivals to the men's companies. The boy-actors (right) did not perform in public, but played to select audiences in candlelit halls, where scenes of bloody murder and ghostly apparitions went down well in the shadows. Talented boys were sometimes kidnapped to join the companies!

▼ **The death of the king, from a 19th-century drawing of *Richard II*.**

In masques, lavish costumes, enery and spectacle were ore important than words.

A 19th-century painting of You Like It. In Shakespeare's day, e girls would have been played boys.

By now he was a wealthy man, with land and investments in Stratford and London. Two years later, in 1603, Queen Elizabeth died and the Scottish king James VI came to England to take the throne. James loved the theatre and granted the Lord Chamberlain's Men a royal charter. From now on they were The King's Men. Their foremost members, including Shakespeare, became Grooms of the Bedchamber – an honorary position at court.

A COUNTRY OUTING

Plague again hit London in 1603 and the actors left town. They were commanded to appear before King James at Wilton House near Salisbury, home of the countess of Pembroke. Family tradition has it that on 3 December they played *As You Like It* and that the countess wrote in a letter 'We have the man Shakespeare with us'. The actors were paid £30. Shakespeare was a good actor, by all accounts, but usually took small parts such as the Ghost in *Hamlet*, old men and kings. He would have been a good understudy, since he knew everyone's lines!

ROBED FOR THE BEDCHAMBER

When James was crowned in 1604, Shakespeare walked in the coronation procession through London wearing his Groom of the Bedchamber red livery. The playwright's name headed the list of actors supplied with four and a half yards of red cloth for the occasion by the Master of the Great Wardrobe.

Over Christmas 1604, James saw his King's Men in eight of Shakespeare's plays, including *Othello* at the Banqueting House in Whitehall, *The Merry Wives of Windsor* and *Measure for Measure*. In spring, he saw *Love's Labour's Lost*, *Henry V* and *Measure for Measure*.

■ END OF THE GLOBE ■

BETWEEN 1604 and 1608, Shakespeare wrote his greatest tragedies: *Othello, King Lear, Macbeth, Antony and Cleopatra* and *Coriolanus. Macbeth*, a play about Scottish history, was no doubt written with King James in mind. The king was a superstitious man, fascinated by witchcraft. In the play, Macbeth is drawn on to kill King Duncan by three witches. Guy Fawkes and his fellow conspirators had just tried to blow up James – a fate that had befallen the king's father, Lord Darnley.

BROTHERS AND PARTNERS

William was not the only Shakespeare in London. His brother Gilbert was a haberdasher (clothes-seller) there, but, like William, kept his old links with Stratford. Younger brother Edmund had become an actor, but not with William's company. He died in London in 1607.

In 1608 Shakespeare's company took over an indoor theatre – the Blackfriars – which they could use during the winter. It had formerly

EVENTS

1606 Puritans get a law passed to ban swearing and blasphemy on stage. Laws also passed against Roman Catholics. Willem Jansz, a Dutch sea captain, sights Australia.
1607 Shakespeare's daughter Susanna marries Dr John Hall. Shakespeare's brother Edmund dies. John Smith founds the English colony of Jamestown in America.
1608 Shakespeare's granddaughter Elizabeth is born. His mother dies. The King's Men move into the Blackfriars theatre for indoor winter performances. French explorer Champlain founds Quebec (in Canada). The telescope is invented.
1610 Galileo uses a telescope to look at the stars. Tea is shipped to Europe.
1611 The Authorized (King James) Version of the Bible is published.
1613 The Globe burns down.

▼ Striking terror into his murderer, the ghost of Banquo appears ingeniously out of a pillar in this Victorian production of Shakespeare's tragedy *Macbeth.*

THE PLAYS

THE DATES are those of the likely first performance of the plays. There is not enough evidence for scholars to be able to agree on actual dates.
1589-91 *Henry VI* (three parts)
1593 *Richard III, The Comedy of Errors*
1594 *Titus Andronicus, The Taming of the Shrew, Two Gentlemen of Verona, Love's Labour's Lost, Romeo and Juliet*
1595 *Richard II, A Midsummer Night's Dream*
1596 *King John, The Merchant of Venice*
1597 *Henry IV* (parts 1 and 2)

▶ The great 18th-century actor David Garrick introduced a more 'natural' style of acting and helped rekindle interest in Shakespeare. Here he is shown playing four of the great tragic heroes.

▼ An indoor playhouse. This 17th-century drawing shows many of the characters and 'turns' that appeared on the stage. Unlike the sunlit open-air theatres, indoor playhouses had chandeliers and footlights to light performances at night.

been used by a company of child-actors, who were popular with fashionable audiences. A new theatre meant more new plays, and now Francis Beaumont and John Fletcher began to write for the King's Men. Fletcher later replaced Shakespeare as the company playwright. The two worked together on *Henry VIII*.

TIME TO GO?

By 1609 Shakespeare was thinking of leaving London, and three years later was back in Stratford, though still writing from time to time. He also kept a business interest in London, buying a house in Blackfriars which he let out. One of his business partners was the landlord of the Mermaid Tavern, where poets and playwrights met to eat, drink and talk. Ben Jonson, John Donne, Beaumont, Fletcher and Sir Walter Raleigh all went there. Shakespeare was famous and popular. *Hamlet* and *Richard II* were even played on board a ship bound for the East Indies in 1607-08. His new plays *The Tempest* and *The Winter's Tale* were played before the king in 1611.

A FIERY END

Shakespeare's play-writing career probably ended when the Globe did. The theatre went out with a bang. On 29 June 1613, *Henry VIII* was in full swing. A cannon was fired and its paper 'shot' set fire to the thatched roof. The blaze destroyed the Globe in less than an hour.

Shakespeare's theatre was gone. Its timbers – as part of the old Theatre – had resounded to his first plays and – as part of the Globe – to his last. When the rebuilt Globe reopened, Shakespeare was back home in Stratford.

▼ A model of the Globe and its surroundings. Amazingly, no lives were lost as the 2000-strong audience fled the burning building in 1613. Fire ripped through the thatched roof but the oak timbers were slower to flame.

■ BACK TO STRATFORD ■

SHAKESPEARE had eased gently into retirement. He kept his interests in London and the theatre, and friends came to visit him in Stratford. In April 1616, Ben Jonson paid him a call. The poet Michael Drayton, who lived nearby, joined them in a 'merrie meeting' at which they drank wine and ate pickled herrings.

Then Shakespeare fell ill. He made his will, and died on 23 April, aged 52. The parish register records the burial two days later of 'Will. Shakespeare, gent.'.

WILL AND HIS PLAYS

Shakespeare left most of his property to his daughter Susanna. He also left small sums to Stratford friends and three in London, including Richard Burbage. He left his wife the 'second-best bed' but by law she would have had a share of the property too.

By 1619, pirated copies of Shakespeare's plays were being printed. The King's Men put a stop to this and determined to have them published accurately. John Heminges and Henry Condell, the actor friends left money by Shakespeare, gathered together his writings and

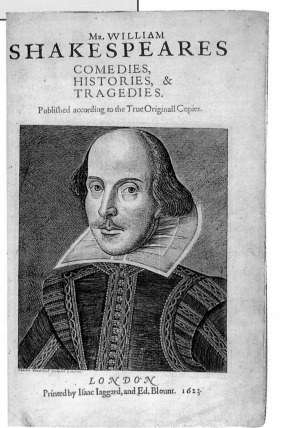

Mr. WILLIAM
SHAKESPEARES
COMEDIES,
HISTORIES, &
TRAGEDIES.
Published according to the True Originall Copies.

LONDON
Printed by Isaac Iaggard, and Ed. Blount. 1623.

◀ The title page of the First Folio, printed in 1623. Gathering the texts of so many plays, and then separating bad pirated texts from true versions was a labour of love for Shakespeare's friends, John Heminges and Henry Condell.

IVDICIO PYLIVM GENIO SOCRATEM,
TERRA TEGIT, POPVLVS MÆRET,

STAY PASSENGER, WHY GOEST THO
READ IF THOV CANST, WHOM ENVIOVS D
WITH IN THIS MONVMENT SHAKSPEARE
QVICK NATVRE DIDE WHOSE NAME, DOTH
FAR MORE, THEN COST: SIEH ALL Y HE
LEAVES LIVING ART, BVT PAGE, TO SE

WHO WAS SHAKESPEARE?

SHAKESPEARE'S plays show such a wide interest and knowledge of the world, and of human nature, that people are amazed they could be the work of one man – and a man with only a free grammar school education. Some doubters have claimed that the plays were written by Christopher Marlowe (after a fake 'death'), by the statesman Francis Bacon, the Earl of Southampton or other noblemen. Some even claim that Queen Elizabeth herself wrote them! The most convincing theory is that Shakespeare's plays were written by Shakespeare.

◀ **This monument to Shakespeare was built near his tomb in Holy Trinity Church a few years after his death. Memorials in Stratford today include several working theatres.**

▶ **Shakespeare wrote his will about a month before his death. He left his home to his daughter, Susanna, but his wife Anne would have continued to live there.**

▼ **Because of the curse inscribed on his tomb, some people think that a secret lies hidden in Shakespeare's grave. It is more likely that he simply did not want people to disturb his bones.**

produced the First Folio of all the plays in 1623 in order 'to keep the memory of so worthy a friend and fellow alive'.

WHAT WAS HE LIKE?

Before Shakespeare's wife Anne died in 1623, a monument to Will had been put up in Stratford church, with a bust of the playwright. People who knew Shakespeare said it was like him. The portrait of him in the First Folio is also said to be a good likeness. The picture known as the Chandos portrait (see page 5) was owned by Shakespeare's godson and may have been painted by Richard Burbage.

From Heminges and Condell, who collected his work, we learn that Shakespeare's 'mind and hand went together; and what he thought, he uttered with that easinesse that we have scarce received from him a blot in his papers'.

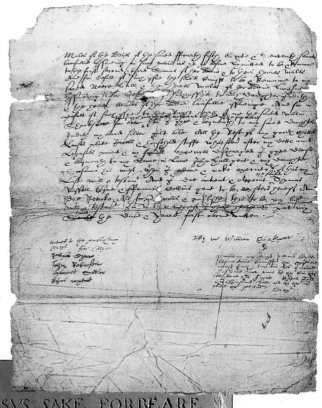

GOOD FREND FOR IESVS SAKE FORBEARE,
TO DIGG THE DVST ENCLOASED HEARE:
BLESE BE Y MAN Y SPARES THES STONES,
AND CVRST BE HE Y MOVES MY BONES.

■ SHAKESPEARE'S LEGACY ■

NEARLY FOUR hundred years after his death, Shakespeare keeps the theatre alive. He gives work to actors, writers, directors, painters, technicians and all who work to put on his plays – on the stage, on television and in the cinema. Even when set at other periods of history or staged in modern dress, Shakespeare's plays still make sense. His lines are spoken all over the world, in many languages.

Thousands of tourists flock each year to see where he lived in Stratford and to watch the plays at the theatres there. There are Shakespeare festivals, Shakespeare seasons, Shakespeare souvenirs. There is a reconstruction of the Globe theatre in London, close to the site of the original.

Shakespeare is the world's greatest playwright and probably the greatest-ever writer. We know little of his life but know what his mind could imagine. He used more English words than any other writer in the language, and made up many of his own. Phrases we use in everyday speech – quick as a flash, light as air, blood burns, cold comfort, small beer, blinking idiot, and many many more – were coined by Shakespeare. People who have never seen or read his plays may quote from them daily.

▲▼ Shakespeare's characters fascinate actors and audiences alike. Many people visit each new production of a play to see how a particular director and cast interpret it. Among famous actors to have played *Richard III* are Edmund Kean (above), David Garrick (below left) and, on stage and film in our own time, Ian McKellen (below).

'My conscience hath a thousand several
    tongues,
And every tongue brings in a several tal
And every tale condemns me for a villa
                                        Richard

SHAKESPEARE IN OUR LANGUAGE

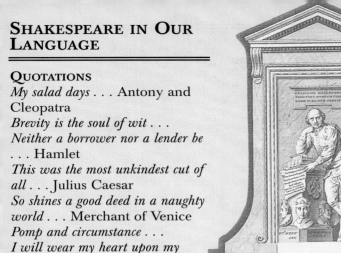

QUOTATIONS

My salad days . . . Antony and Cleopatra
Brevity is the soul of wit . . .
Neither a borrower nor a lender be . . . Hamlet
This was the most unkindest cut of all . . . Julius Caesar
So shines a good deed in a naughty world . . . Merchant of Venice
Pomp and circumstance . . .
I will wear my heart upon my sleeve . . . Othello
O brave new world . . . The Tempest
If music be the food of love, play on . . . Twelfth Night
And thereby hangs a tale . . . As You Like It

EVERYDAY PHRASES

I have not slept one wink. Cymbeline
More in sorrow than in anger.
Time is out of joint.
Cruel only to be kind. Hamlet
All our yesterdays.
What's done is done.
(He hath) eaten me out of house and home. Macbeth
Men of few words. Henry V
It was Greek to me. Julius Caesar
But love is blind. Merchant of Venice
What's in a name? Romeo and Juliet
Cold comfort King John

◄ **Shakespeare's monument in Westminster Abbey. His living memorial is the richness of the English language.**

A new Globe. Audiences can relive the experience of Shakespeare's theatre at the reconstructed Globe, built near the site of the original. It opened in 1997 with a production of *Henry V*, as did the old Globe in 1599. Modern groundlings (right) stand where their forerunners did, in the pit.

■ GLOSSARY ■

ALDERMAN A senior member of a town council, elected by other members usually after long service.

APPRENTICE A young man learning a trade; an apprenticeship in the service of an experienced master could last up to seven years.

APRON In the theatre, part of the stage that sticks out in front of the arch.

BAILIFF A land-agent or estate manager.

BAITING Letting dogs fight tethered bulls or bears for entertainment.

BANNS Public announcement of a proposed wedding, read out in church.

BLANK VERSE Unrhymed verse with lines of five two-syllable 'feet'.

BOROUGH TASTER Town official whose job was to check the quality of local bread and other foods.

BUTTS Mounds behind targets.

CHAPMEN A travelling seller of cheap goods.

CLOWN In Shakespeare's time, clown could mean a country simpleton or a professional comedian.

COMPANY A group of actors working, and travelling, together.

CONSTABLE A local law officer, rather like a village policeman.

COURT The people who live and work with a monarch, and the royal buildings.

COURTIER Member of the court, usually a noble.

CROSSTALK Quickfire conversation between two actors, usually full of jokes.

CUTPURSE A pickpocket or street thief.

DEDICATE To set apart something for a purpose; to address a book or play to an individual, as a mark of respect.

DUMB-SHOW Play without words, mimes.

DUNGHILL A rubbish heap, where human waste might (or might not) be left.

FENCERS Sword-fighters, people who show off their swordsmanship.

GRAMMAR Rules of language and writing.

GRAMMAR SCHOOL Boys' schools in Tudor England, where Latin grammar was taught, and from which many later schools evolved.

GREEK Language spoken in Greece; in Shakespeare's time, scholars studied the language of the Ancient Greeks.

GROUNDLINGS People who paid the cheapest prices to stand in a theatre.

GUILD An association of craftsmen or merchants to which the different craftsmen and merchants had to belong to obtain work in a town.

GUILD HALL Building put up by a guild for its meeting and banquets.

HABERDASHER A dealer in ribbons and small items of clothing.

HORNBOOK A child's schoolbook, made from a single sheet protected by transparent horn.

HUGUENOTS French Protestants, some of whom sought refuge in England from religious persecution.

INN A place where travellers could stay, often built around an open courtyard.

LATIN Language of Ancient Romans, still used in Shakespeare's time as the language of scholars.

LICENCE Permit needed for various purposes, including the performance of a play or for a marriage.

LIVERY Distinctive uniforms worn by servants of a great household or by members of a guild.

LORD CHAMBERLAIN The person responsible for entertainment at court.

LORD MAYOR The chief citizen of London and other important cities; the elected leader of the council.

MASQUES Entertainments with songs, music and acting, often performed in great houses.

NOBLE A person from a rich or important family usually with a title, such as Duke, Earl, Lord, etc.

PAGEANT A dramatic entertainment, often to mark some important event, when people dress up to re-enact stories from history.

PATRONS Rich people who encourage artists and writers by giving them employment or paying for plays to be put on and poems published.

PIT The ground floor of a theatre

PLAGUE A deadly contagious disease carried by fleas from black rats; epidemics of plague killed thousands of people from the 14th to the 17th centuries.

PLAYER Actor.

PLAYHOUSE Theatre.

POACHING Illegally hunting game animals, such as rabbits or deer.

PROPS Short for properties; stage equipment, such as furniture and weapons, that can be moved about.

PURITAN A Christian who follows a simple way of life and a strict form of worship.

QUACK Short for quacksalver, a fake doctor who sold useless medicines (salves), claiming miracle cures for almost anything.

SHARER A person who invests money in a theatre or other venture in return for a share of the profits.

SHORTHAND Quick form of writing.

SPANISH ARMADA Invasion fleet sent by Spain to attack England.

STROLLING PLAYER An actor who wandered from town to town.

TABOR A small drum; the player struck the tabor with one hand, while playing a pipe held in the other.

TIRING HOUSE Room in which actors dressed for the play and stored props.

TOUR To go from town to town performing plays.

TUDOR Family name of the dynasty to which Elizabeth I belonged, founded by Henry VII.

TUTOR A private teacher, employed to teach children at home.

TYBURN Place of execution in London, where Marble Arch now stands.

UNDERSTUDY Actor who learns another's part so that he or she can act as a stand-in.

PLACES TO VISIT

Any performance of any Shakespeare play anywhere.

Anne Hathaway's Cottage,
Shottery, Warwickshire.
Home of Shakespeare's bride.

Hall's Croft,
Stratford-upon-Avon, Warwickshire
Home of Shakespeare's daughter.

Holy Trinity Church,
Stratford-upon-Avon, Warwickshire.

International Shakespeare's Globe Centre,
Bankside, London.
This includes the Globe theatre, exhibition and education department.

Mary Arden's House and Shakespeare Countryside Museum,
Wilmcote, Warwickshire.
Home of Shakespeare's mother.

Nash's House and New Place,
Stratford-upon-Avon, Warwickshire.
Site and grounds of Shakespeare's last house.

National Portrait Gallery,
London.
Portraits of Shakespeare and many of his contemporaries.

Poets' Corner, Westminster Abbey,
London.

Royal Shakespeare Theatre, Swan Theatre and The Other Place,
Stratford-upon-Avon, Warwickshire.
For performances of plays by Shakespeare and other playwrights.

Shakespeare's Birthplace,
The Shakespeare Centre,
Stratford-upon-Avon, Warwickshire.
Shakespeare's birthplace and an exhibition of his life and background.